You Matter

HEALING WITH NATURE

Nikki Roy

 FriesenPress

One Printers Way
Altona, MB R0G 0B0
Canada

www.friesenpress.com

Copyright © 2022 by Nikki Roy
First Edition — 2022

Illustrator: Kate Zessel

All rights reserved.

Disclaimer: Although I am a therapist, I am not your therapist. This book is not a replacement for therapy, rather an individual tool to gently prompt self reflection and growth. Please connect with your own therapist to further discuss anything that comes up for you.

No part of this publication may be reproduced in any form, or by any means, electronic or mechanical, including photocopying, recording, or any information browsing, storage, or retrieval system, without permission in writing from FriesenPress.

ISBN
978-1-03-915253-3 (Hardcover)
978-1-03-915252-6 (Paperback)
978-1-03-915254-0 (eBook)

1. SELF-HELP, PERSONAL GROWTH

Distributed to the trade by The Ingram Book Company

Welcome. Thank you for being here. This book is so special to me as it uniquely blends my two passions: helping others connect to their authentic selves and being present and explorative in nature. I started taking my video and photography interests more seriously when I was in the depths of grad school, struggling to stay afloat and trying to find any source of calm. I texted my mom, asked if she could take me on a photo trip to the mountains, and allow me to borrow one of her cameras to further explore and play around with. I had no idea just how important and impactful that trip would be to my mental health and creative expression. The journey that led me to where I am today in my photo business, also led me to a journey of connection.

My counselling background allows me to foster emotion, connection, safety, and narrative, while my photography allows me to fuel creativity, see perspective, and find the importance of being present. I hope this book can guide you to explore all the wonderful parts of yourself while helping you identify your needs, desires, and dreams. To provide a space where we allow ourselves to show up imperfectly. We all have needs, and we all deserve connection and healing. My hope as you go through this book is that you can pause, breathe, gain insight into your life, and slowly start to regain connection to yourself. After all, the strongest connections we have are those with other human beings, animals, nature, and ourselves. Enjoy. ☺

I will always believe that a genuine and authentic connection is more important than any response.

Every time I go into nature I feel immense gratitude to the people, animals, and environments that came before me. I have an enormous amount of privilege and I can only hope to use some of that to amplify and identify the indigenous people and land that these photos were taken on. Let this acknowledgement serve as a reminder of ongoing efforts to recognize, honour, reconcile, and partner with the Indigenous people of Turtle Island whose lands and water we all benefit from today.

Let's start with an affirmation:

Right here, right now, I am more than enough. Take a deep breath. Let's begin!

This picture was taken on the land of the Stz'uminus, S'òlh Téméxw and Coast Salish people.

This picture was taken on the land of the Hul'qumi'num Treaty Group, Stz'uminus, S'òlh Téméxw, and Coast Salish people.

Journal Prompt:

Reflect on a time when you felt genuinely happy and joyful. Who was there? What were you doing? Where in your body did you feel joy? What colour is joy for you? What was happening that day?

This picture was taken on the land of the Stz'uminus, S'òlh Téméxw and Coast Salish people.

This picture was taken on the land of the nuučaaṅuuɫʔatḥ nisma (Nuu-chah-nulth) and ƛaʔuukʷiʔatḥ (Tla-o-qui-aht) people.

Affirmation:

It's natural to need others, to seek belonging, and to desire connection.

Connection Seeking:

Reach out to a trusted person and tell them two ways they have influenced your life in a positive, encouraging, or supportive manner. What did they do? How do they make you feel? Is it safety, belonging, connection, or freedom?

This picture was taken on the land of the Hul'qumi'num Treaty Group, Stz'uminus, S'òlh Téméxw, and Coast Salish people.

This picture was taken on the land of the Hul'qumi'num Treaty Group, Stz'uminus, S'òlh Téméxw, and Coast Salish people.

Journal Prompt:

All emotions come with a message; it's our job to understand the information it's carrying. Connect with a specific emotion you have felt strongly in the last week. Name it, write it down, and become curious about it. Explore what that emotion is trying to tell you. Where do you feel it in your body? What does this emotion need? Is it comfort, safety, connection, or communication?

TIP: Use the emotion wheel attached to the back of this book. This wheel can help you identify the emotions you are truly feeling. The closer you can get to the accurate emotion, the higher chance you have of processing it effectively.

This picture was taken on the land of the Kwanlin Dün and Ta'an Kwäch'än Dënéndeh people.

This picture was taken on the land of the Kwanlin Dün
and Ta'an Kwäch'än Dënéndeh people.

Affirmation:

I give myself permission to stumble, fall, and feel imperfection.
I will honour my truth today.

Connection Seeking:

Put your phone on airplane mode for one hour and read a book, do yoga, meditate, cook, walk, or do whatever that brings you a sense of calm and peace. Notice what comes up for you in this intentional hour of connection to your soul.

This picture was taken on the land of the Ucluelet people.

This picture was taken on the land of the Hul'qumi'num Treaty Group, Stz'uminus, S'òlh Téméxw, and Coast Salish people.

Journal Prompt:

Reflect on all the ways you connect with nature. Do you enjoy the looks of it? The smell of it? Where do you feel most at peace within nature? What do you notice about yourself when immersed in it?

This picture was taken on the land of the Ktunaxa, ʔamakʔis, and Secwepemcúl'ecw (Secwépemc) people.

This picture was taken on the land of the nuučaańuułʔatḥ nism̓a (Nuu-chah-nulth) and ƛaʔuukʷiʔatḥ (Tla-o-qui-aht) people.

Affirmation:

Reminder: being present is a practice and one I will prioritize.

Connection Seeking:

Be present with an animal; tune into how they use their senses to experience their world. Watch them, pet them, admire them, play with them, and laugh with them. I invite you to reflect on how animals use their intuition and senses to provide for themselves and keep themselves safe. How does this connect to you? How have you pushed away your own intuition to meet others' expectations and needs of you?

This picture was taken on the land of the nuučaańuutʔath nisma (Nuu-chah-nulth) and ƛaʔuukʷiʔatḥ (Tla-o-qui-aht) people.

This picture was taken on the land of the Coast Salish, səl̓ilwətaʔɬ təməxʷ (Tsleil-Waututh), Skwxwú7mesh-ulh Temíx̱w (Squamish), S'ólh Téméxw (Stó:lō), and šxʷməθkʷəy̓əmaʔɬ təməxʷ (Musqueam) people.

Journal Prompt:

This is a tough one. I am giving you so much empathy and compassion as you reflect on this prompt, as it can be painful and eye-opening. Explore and write down all the ways you have been trying to please other people. Give yourself permission to release the pressures, burdens, and expectations that others have on you.

This picture was taken on the land of the Hul'qumi'num Treaty Group, Stz'uminus, S'òlh Téméxw, and Coast Salish people.

This picture was taken on the land of the Hul'qumi'num Treaty Group, Stz'uminus, S'òlh Téméxw, and Coast Salish people.

Affirmation:

I am allowed to change my opinions, feelings, and thoughts as I grow and evolve.

Connection Seeking:

Let's talk about the five love languages. If you haven't heard of them yet, they consist of quality time, acts of service, physical touch, gifts, and words of affirmation. One of the most powerful things we can do for ourselves is learning how to give and show ourselves love by using our own love language. Do something for yourself that aligns with your love language.

For example:

- Quality time: Plan a day where you spend quality time with yourself (or a pet). This can include being outside, trying a new activity, or spending time doing things you feel most at peace with.

- Acts of service: Make a list of activities or things you have been putting off and want to do for yourself and check them off as you go. This could be things like cooking your favourite meal or booking appointments that you have put off.

- Physical touch: Book a massage, take a bath, exfoliate/wash/moisturize, spend time in nature, and touch and feel the different elements.

- Gifts: Get yourself a thoughtful gift that makes you feel more at peace with yourself.

- Words of affirmation: Write yourself a letter, write down affirmations, or write a poem.

Chapman, G. D. (2010). The five love languages. Walker Large Print.

This picture was taken on the land of the nuučaan̓ uuɬʔatḥ nism̓ a (Nuu-chah-nulth), and ƛaʔuukʷiʔatḥ (Tla-o-qui-aht) people.

This picture was taken on the land of the nuučaaṅuuł?atḥ nisma (Nuu-chah-nulth) and ƛa?uukʷi?atḥ (Tla-o-qui-aht) people.

Journal Prompt:

Reflect on a feeling, thought, or opinion you have had in your life that has changed due to your evolution as a human. Where did it come from in the first place? Who taught you this? What influenced this? How does this changed feeling/thought/opinion better align with who you are today? How does this serve you?

This picture was taken on the land of the Nłeʔkepmx Tmíxʷ (Nlaka'pamux), Syilx tmixʷ (Okanagan), and Confederated Tribes of the Colville Reservation.

This picture was taken on the land of the Coast Salish and S'ólh Téméxw (Stó:lō) people.

Affirmation:

When I feel lost, I trust that I am being led to greater things.

Connection Seeking:

Practice being present with yourself. How are you feeling today? Did you meet your needs today? What is one thing you are experiencing in this moment? Physical, emotional, or sensual?

TIP: Go somewhere quiet, place your hand on your heart, your arm, or your leg (whatever is comfy), and practice box breathing. Breathe in for four seconds, hold for four seconds, breathe out for four seconds, and hold for four seconds. Take deep belly breaths. Repeat until you feel connected with your body.

This picture was taken on the land of the nuučaaṅuutʔatḥ nisma (Nuu-chah-nulth) and ƛaʔuukʷiʔatḥ (Tla-o-qui-aht) people.

This picture was taken on the land of the nuučaaṅuułʔatḥ nisḿa (Nuu-chah-nulth) and ƛaʔuukʷiʔatḥ (Tla-o-qui-aht) people.

Journal Prompt:

Write down five self-compassion statements to yourself.

TIP: It can be awkward and difficult to begin writing self-compassion statements because many of us were taught to shame ourselves when experiencing pain. A self-compassion statement can be acknowledging when things feel hard, having your own back, validating your feelings, and allowing room for learning. Now you try!

This picture was taken on the land of the nuučaańuułʔatḥ nisma (Nuu-chah-nulth) and ƛaʔuukʷiʔatḥ (Tla-o-qui-aht) people.

This picture was taken on the land of the Niitsítpiis-stahkoii ᖹᐟᖻᐦᒣᑯᐧ (Blackfoot / Niitsítapi ᖹᐟᒣᑯ), Ktunaxa ʔamakʔis, Stoney, Tsuu T'ina, and Michif Piyii (Métis) people.

Affirmation:

Shame will never motivate me long term; self-compassion is the key to growth.

Connection Seeking:

Write a short one-page letter to yourself using themes of self-compassion, apology, kindness, acceptance, and understanding. Unconditionally accept yourself. Give yourself permission to move through. Forgive yourself for past mistakes. Provide your younger "you" some grace and forgiveness. Allow yourself to see the human in you. Provide hope, love, and acceptance to yourself.

This picture was taken on the land of the Niitsítpiis-stahkoii ᖹᐟᒧᐧᐨᑯᐧᑌ (Blackfoot / Niitsítapi ᖹᐟᒧᐧᑯ), Ktunaxa ʔamakʔis, Stoney, Tsuu T'ina, and Michif Piyii (Métis) people.

This picture was taken on the land of the Niitsítpiis-stahkoii ᓂᐥᓱᐧᒃᖻᐧ (Blackfoot / Niitsítapi ᓂᐥᓱᐧᑕᑯ), Ktunaxa ʔamakʔis, Stoney, Tsuu T'ina, and Michif Piyii (Métis) people.

Journal Prompt:

Let's work on writing down your needs. This includes physical, mental, and emotional. This might be difficult because we are often told to dismiss our own needs for the sake of others. I want to validate how normal and okay that is. It's okay for you to feel awkward when identifying your needs, and it's important for you to work through this block. There is no right or wrong way to identify these. When our emotions are met with what is needed, they will often process and move through us on their own. (Use your emotion wheel here!)

For example:

- When I am sad, I need to feel comfort and safety.
- When I am angry, I need to be alone to process my emotions, and then I need clarity to move on.
- I need to feel respected and valued by the people in my life.
- Now your turn!

This picture was taken on the land of the O'odham Jeweḍ and Hia-Ced O'odham people.

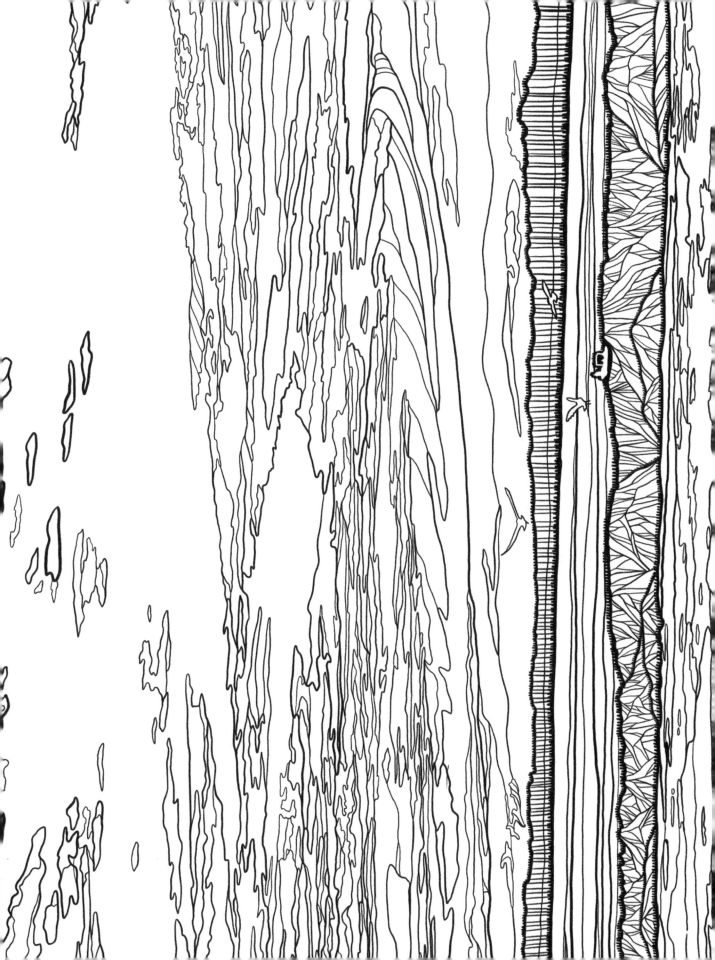

This picture was taken on the land of the Ucluelet people.

Affirmation:

My needs matter. My needs deserve attention. My needs deserve to be met.

Connection Seeking:

Go hug a tree! Observe it. Watch how it stands tall, spreads its roots, and isn't afraid to demand space. Watch it move with the wind, provide a home for smaller animals, and connect to all other living things. Reflect on how the tree met its needs. How did it identify what it needed and work to get it?

TIP: Serotonin (our happy hormone) is a physiologically active amine which is a well-known neurotransmitter that regulates mood, sleep, and anxiety in mammals. We know, through research, that parts of plant species, including leaves, stems, roots, fruits, and seeds, contain quantities of serotonin. So, hugging, interacting, touching, breathing, and feeling plants can help boost and regulate mood while also keeping us grounded!

Ramakrishna, A., Giridhar, P., & Ravishankar, G. A. (2011). Phytoserotonin: a review. Plant signaling & behavior, 6(6), 800–809. https://doi.org/10.4161/psb.6.6.15242

This picture was taken on the land of the Coast Salish and S'ólh Téméxw (Stó:lō) people.

Mindfulness Technique:

Sit down somewhere quiet and place your hand on your heart. Take five deep breaths in, and five longer, slower, deep breaths out. Repeat out loud: Right here, right now, I am enough.

Tune into your hearing sense and listen to what is around you. Tune into your feeling sense, and touch your skin, your clothes, and the surface you are sitting on. Tune into your smell and deeply smell what is around you. What can you taste? Perhaps a drink or a snack? And lastly, tune into your sight and choose a colour; try to find three things in that colour.

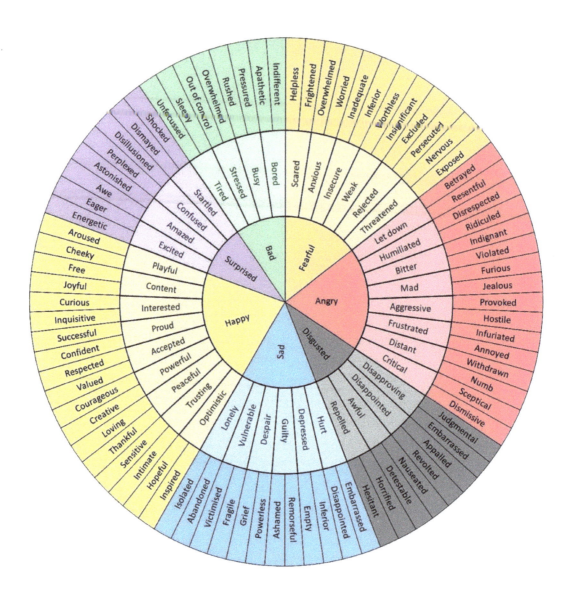

It's never too late to find your way back to yourself, to heal wounds, or to pursue a new version of you.

You, right now, matter. You are enough just as you are. Your value and worthiness in this world are not defined by your successes, looks, or achievements. You deserve all the wonderful gifts of healing, emotion, and connection to all.

About the Author

Nikki Roy, MA, CCC, is a Certified Canadian Counsellor who practices community mental health and private practice. Nikki is passionate about making mental health more accessible, normalized, and empowering. After all, we don't always need a traditional counselling space to foster healing.

Growing up with parents who had cameras permanently attached to their hands, Nikki naturally came to a point in her life where she too found a sense of calm, passion, and creative expression being behind the lens. As you make your way through this book, you will see a wonderful combination of both Nikki, and her mothers, photographs.

Nikki now resides with her husband, Colton, in White Rock, BC, with their two fur babies, Hawk and Jonesy.

CPSIA information can be obtained
at www.ICGtesting.com
Printed in the USA
JSHW070325070723
43767JS00002BA/3